CW00537427

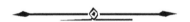

ISBN 978-0-266-16787-7
PIBN 10103278

# CATALOGUE

OF A

## COLLECTION OF ENGRAVED AND OTHER PORTRAITS OF

# LINCOLN

EXHIBITED AT

## THE GROLIER CLUB
### NEW YORK

Twenty-nine East Thirty-second Street

Saturday, April 8th, to Saturday, April 22d

1899

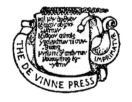

THE DE VINNE PRESS

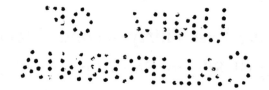

# INTRODUCTION.

## By Charles Henry Hart.

THIS catalogue is the first attempt to make a systematic record of the engraved portraits of Abraham Lincoln, sixteenth President of the United States; and never before, as far as can be ascertained, has a special exhibition of them been undertaken. The catalogue and exhibition therefore are not only interesting, but they are important; for while completeness is not claimed for either, they will undoubtedly serve to stimulate interest in the subject and lead to the unearthing of portraits of Lincoln hitherto unknown. Such is universally the result of a first essay in any new field of investigation, which, at best, can only be regarded as a tentative effort, and therefore is entitled to the consideration due to all pioneer work, commendation for what has been done and forbearance for that which unconsciously has been left undone.

Mr. Lincoln came to the forefront comparatively so late in life, when the art of engraving had fallen into disuse, that but little variety will be found in the types of the portraits shown, and but few of them possess any artistic merit. Yet their value as human documents is unmistakable, and this will increase as time rolls on; for Abraham Lincoln is the typical American in history, and consequently he is the greatest of *Americans*. Washington, who made Lincoln possible, was historically a Briton, so that when we place the saviour of his country upon the lofty pedestal we do, we in no wise disparage or detract from the eminence of him who was " first in war, first in peace, and first in the hearts of his countrymen,"— the father of his country.

Abraham Lincoln was born in Hardin, now Larue county, Kentucky, near Nolin creek, about a couple of miles from Hodgensville, the present county seat of Larue county, on the 12th day of February, 1809. His parents were poor and illiterate, and the education he received was meagre, his early life being one of continued hardships. It was not long, however, before Lincoln showed that he was *sui generis*. At the age of twenty-four he secured the office of country postmaster, and the next year entered the Illinois legislature, where he sat through four sessions. He read law and was admitted to the bar, and at thirty-seven was sent to Congress, where he served for one term. Consequently he had acquired some local reputation, but his name was unknown to the country at large, until he entered the field of debate with Stephen A. Douglas, in the summer of 1858, both being candidates for a seat in the United States Senate. This led the way to his famous speech at the Cooper Institute, New York, on February 27, 1860, which Horace Greeley stamped as the best political speech to which he ever listened, defining a political speech to be, "an effort to convince the largest possible number that they ought to be on the speaker's side, not on the other." Therefore when, in May of 1860, Abraham Lincoln was nominated for the Presidency, the politicians of the country knew, if the people did not, something of what manner of man he was. His subsequent election, career, and foul murder are matter of history too familiar to need repeating, but this brief outline of the life of the man whose portraiture is exhibited at this time will explain why his portraits cover such a short period of his life.

At the time of his nomination for the Presidency, Mr. Lincoln gave this description of himself: "I am in height six feet four inches nearly; lean in flesh, weighing on an average 180 pounds; dark complexion, with coarse black hair and gray eyes." To this description his secretary, Mr. Nicolay, adds these details of the peculiarities of Lincoln's form and features: " Large head with high crown of skull; thick, bushy hair; large and deep eye caverns; heavy eyebrows; a large nose; large ears; large mouth; very high and prominent cheek bones; cheeks thin and sunken; strongly developed jaw bones; chin slightly upturned; a thin but sinewy neck, rather long; long arms; large hands; chest thin and narrow as compared with great height; legs of more than proportionate length, and large feet."

While these structural particulars are of value and have been utilized by Mr. St. Gaudens in the most masterly statue yet erected in America, alone they would give no idea of how Abraham Lincoln appeared, in the flesh, to those who knew him. And indeed no word-painting can convey to the mind of another an adequate conception of the appearance of any person, so much depends upon the spirit and expression, which latter, in persons of character, is ever changing. With Mr. Lincoln this was notably the case, so that it was the despair of painters and of photographers to catch a likeness, and the best that can be done is to make a composite, in the mind, from all the pictures that we have of him and all the characteristics that we know of him.

Mr. Lincoln has been called by one of his best friends " an ugly, awkward giant." But no man with the soulful expression that flowed from his eyes could be ugly, and that evanescent, subtle quality which was supreme in him, is the most difficult to catch and fix.

If to-day any one wants to behold Abraham Lincoln, as he was when he lived and moved and had his being, at his full stature and with his noble soul astir, journey to Chicago and kneel before the bronze statue by Augustus St. Gaudens. It is the man himself, with all his humility and nobility, with all his gentleness and strength; " With malice toward none, with charity for all, with firmness in the right as God gives us to see the right." It is not Abraham Lincoln the liberator of slaves, but Abraham Lincoln the Saviour of the Union,— he who said, " My paramount object in this struggle is to save the Union, and is not either to save or to destroy slavery." And these words are inscribed at the base of St. Gaudens's statue, showing the lofty and true historic conception of the man possessed by this great sculptor.

The earliest portrait of Lincoln painted from life was by Thomas Hicks, who was sent for the purpose from New York to Springfield soon after the nomination. It is a full bust, nearly in profile, and portrays Lincoln without any beard, an adornment or disfigurement he never wore until after his election to the Presidency. Life-portraits of him were also painted by William Morris Hunt, E. D. Marchant, G. P. A. Healy, A. J. Conant, Frank B.

Carpenter, and Matthew Wilson; a miniature on ivory was painted by J. Henry Brown, and is now in the possession of Hon. Robert T. Lincoln; and Leonard W. Volk, of Chicago, and Thomas D. Jones, of Columbus, each made busts of him from life. Volk also made, as likewise did Clark Mills, a mask from the living face; but life masks such as these are of little or no value as portraits. Indeed so true is this, that when Mr. St. Gaudens saw the cast from Clark Mills's mask of Lincoln, he insisted that it must be a death mask, so lacking is it in vitality.

The best prints of Lincoln, in an artistic sense, are the etchings by Rajon and Johnson, the large woodcut by Kruell, and the line-engravings by Marshall and Gugler. That by Gugler is claimed to be the largest portrait ever engraved on steel. It purports to be from a painting by J. H. Littlefield, a former student at law in Mr. Lincoln's office; but the portrait is in fact from a Brady photograph, with a slight change in the arrangement of the hair. While prints, including those on steel, wood, and stone, are the principal objects shown in the present exhibition, perhaps the only satisfactory study of the portraiture of Abraham Lincoln can be made from photographs, of which there are many, taken within the last five years of his life.

Interest in everything pertaining to Lincoln is on the steady increase, and many valuable collections have been formed of his portraits, of the literature pertaining to him, and of personal memorials.

The Lincoln cult is only in its infancy. It has had but a single generation in which to grow; but as the perspective of time brings into grander relief the noble proportions of its subject, homage and admiration for him will be bounded only by the civilized world.

The Committee of Arrangements desires to thank Major W. H. Lambert and Mr. W. C. Crane, who are not members of the Grolier Club, for their valuable contributions, without which the exhibition could not have been completed.

# ENGRAVINGS.

The inscriptions are always at the bottom, unless otherwise stated.

"Facsimile signature" is abbreviated "Fac. sig."

The sizes are in inches, the width being given first. Whenever possible, the size of the full plate is given, as well as that of the engraved part.

In the case of vignette-portraits, the greatest width and height of the engraved part of the plate are noted.

"L. P." before the size means that only Lincoln's portrait has been measured, and not the remainder of the engraving.

# PORTRAITS.

## Anonymous.

1. Line.   Bust; beard; directed, facing and looking to the right.   India paper.   Inscription, centre: *Abraham Lincoln.*

$1\frac{5}{8}$ x 2.   Plate, 3 x 4.

2. Line.   Bust; beard; directed, facing and looking to the right.   $\frac{9}{16}$ x $\frac{11}{16}$.   Plate, $2\frac{7}{16}$ x 3.

3. Line. Bust; beard; profile to right. Inscription, centre: *A. Lincoln.* | *Manhattan Engraving Company, New York.*          $1\frac{1}{4}$ x $1\frac{1}{2}$.

4. Line. Bust; beard; directed to the front, facing and looking slightly to the right. Proof. India paper. "323" engraved under left shoulder.          $1\frac{5}{8}$ x $1\frac{3}{4}$.    Plate, $2\frac{7}{16}$ x $2\frac{15}{16}$.

   Pencil note on margin: "U. S. Treasury Dept. After Carpenter."

5. Line. Bust; beard; directed, facing and looking slightly to the right. Oval, with ornamental border on bottom and sides.

   $1\frac{1}{2}$ x $1\frac{15}{16}$.    Plate, $2\frac{15}{16}$ x $4\frac{9}{16}$.

   *A.* Proof, with "Lincoln" engraved in border, underneath.

   *B.* With inscription below, centre: *Abraham Lincoln.* | *Bureau, Engraving & Printing.*

6. Line and stipple. Bust; beard (closely cropped); directed very slightly to the left, facing and looking to the front. A bit of curtain with tassel on the right. In oval border, enclosing a line of stars, and surrounded by decoration, with an eagle above, and a view of the Capitol and military below, with title in the border: *Capitol — Washington.* Inscription, centre: *A. Lincoln* [fac. sig.] | *Published by B. B. Russell & Co.,* 55 *Cornhill, Boston.*          $3\frac{13}{16}$ x $5\frac{1}{4}$.

7. Line. Bust; beard; directed, facing and looking to the right. Inscription, centre: *Abraham
Lincoln | Präsident der Nord-Amerikanischen
Staaten | Meuchelmörderisch geschossen den
14ten April, 1865 | am nächsten Tag gestorben.*
$2\frac{1}{4} \times 2\frac{3}{4}$. Plate, $3\frac{1}{8} \times 4\frac{3}{4}$.

8. Line and stipple. Full-length, seated; beard;
directed to the left, facing and looking very
slightly to the right. Hands resting on vol-
ume placed on left leg; left foot on torn papers. Drapery in background passing before
column and over table on left. Bust of Wash-
ington on column at right. $5\frac{1}{2} \times 7\frac{3}{4}$.

*A.* With inscription, centre: *A. Lincoln* [fac.
sig.] | *Fry & Co., Publishers, New York |
Entered according to act of Congress A. D.
1862 by Johnson, Fry & Co.. . . N. Y.*
—left: *Painted by*— right: *Alonzo Chap-
pel.*

*B.* Papers under left foot are now lettered
"Jef Davis Secession" and "Southern
Confederacy." Inscription, added, after
the "A. Lincoln" in facsimile: *Likeness
?from a recent Photograph?from life.*

*C.* Another head has been substituted; heavier
features, hair now falling over forehead
towards right eye instead of towards left;
eyes have an upward glance. Directed,
facing and looking as before.

9. Mixed. Bust; beard; directed and facing to the right, looking to the front. Inscription, centre: *Western Engraving Co. Chicago.*

$3\frac{5}{8} \times 4\frac{3}{8}.$

10. Line. Bust; beard; directed, facing and looking to the right. Printed at head of " Proclamation of Emancipation" engraved in very small characters. Inscription under the Proclamation, in minute letters: *Entered according to act of Congress in the year* 1864 *by A. Kidder in . . . New York McLees* 609 *Broadway.* L. P., $\frac{1}{2} \times \frac{5}{8}$. The whole Proclamation,

$2\frac{3}{4} \times 3\frac{3}{4}.$

11. Line. Bust; beard; directed, facing and looking to the right. Printed at left end of blank check of the First National Bank of Mattoon, Illinois, 186 –. *Western Engraving Co. Chicago.*                    L. P., $1\frac{7}{16} \times 1\frac{3}{4}.$

12. Line and stipple. Half-length, seated; beard; directed slightly to left, facing and looking to the right. Right hand holding Emancipation Proclamation, left arm resting on book placed over paper on table. Column to the left. Inscription, centre: *Entered according to act of Congress A. D.* 1870, *by Johnson, Fry & Co. . . . N. Y. | A. Lincoln* [fac. sig.] | *From the original painting by Chappel, in*

*the possession of the publishers. | Johnson, Wilson & Co. Publishers, New York.* 5½ x 7⅜.

13. Line. Full-length, seated; beard; directed, facing and looking to the right. Right arm resting on arm of chair; left hand holding papers on knees. To the right, a table filled with books and papers, behind which is a bust of Washington in front of a window with curtains. Inscription, centre: *A. Lincoln* [fac. sig.] | *From the original painting by Nast, in the possession of the Publishers | Johnson, Fry & Co. Publishers, New York. | Entered according to act of Congress A. D.* 1866 *by Johnson, Fry & Co. . . . New York.* 5½ x 7⅜.

14. Line. Bust; beard; directed slightly to the left, facing slightly to the right, looking to the front. In oval border. Similar portraits, a trifle smaller, of Grant above, Sheridan (full beard) below to the left, Sherman below to the right. Eagle and seven American flags over Grant; war scenes form a background. Name of subject appears under each portrait. Inscription, centre: *Published by* | *H. H. Lloyd & Co.* 21 *John St. New York.*

L. P., 1¾ x 2⁵⁄₁₆.

15. Mixed. Bust; beard; directed, facing and looking to the right. Inscription, centre: *President Lincoln.* 1¾ x 2¼.

"From Photo by Fredricks."

16. Mixed. Bust; beard; directed to the right,
facing and looking almost to the front. Inscription, centre [facsimile autograph]: *Yours
truly | A. Lincoln.*                    $4\frac{1}{8}$ x $5\frac{5}{8}$.

17. Mixed. Shown to the waist; beard; directed,
facing and looking to the right. Inscription,
centre: *Abraham Lincoln | President of U. S.
A. | A. Lincoln* [fac. sig.] | *New York.   G. P.
Putnam.*                               $4\frac{3}{8}$ x 5.

18. Mixed. Full-length. Inscription, centre: *Abraham Lincoln* [fac. sig.].              $7\frac{1}{2}$ x 11.
   For description, see No. 30, of which this is a smaller
   copy, by another hand.

## Burt, Chas.

19. Line. Bust; beard; directed to the front,
facing and looking slightly to the right. Proof;
no inscription.     $3\frac{5}{8}$ x $4\frac{7}{8}$.   Plate, $7\frac{1}{2}$ x 11.

20. Line. Bust; beard; directed, facing and looking slightly to the right. Oval border lightly
indicated. Proof before all letters; unfinished.
                          $1\frac{5}{8}$ x $2\frac{1}{8}$.   Plate, 3 x $4\frac{3}{8}$.

## Buttre, J. C.

21. Mixed. Bust; clean-shaven; directed to the
right, facing very slightly to the right, looking
to the front.     $5\frac{1}{8}$ x $5\frac{1}{2}$.   Plate, $6\frac{3}{8}$ x $9\frac{3}{8}$.
   *A.* Proof. Outline; shadows indicated; cross-
   hatching on body.

*B*. Finished plate. Inscription, centre: *A. Lincoln* [fac. sig.]—left: *Photograph by M. B. Brady*—right: *Engd. by J. C. Buttre, N. Y(*

*C*. Central portion of same, printed on strip of satin in shape of a campaign badge.

*D*. Same. Plate as published in a book. Inscription as before, and below, in centre: *Published by J. C. Buttre*, 48 *Franklin St. N. York.*

22. Mixed. Bust; clean-shaven; directed to the right, facing very slightly to the right, looking to the front. $4\frac{3}{8}$ x $4\frac{3}{4}$.

*A*. Proof, etched in outline.

*B*. Finished plate. Inscription, centre: *A. Lincoln* [fac. sig.]—left: *Photograph by Brady*—right: *Engd. by J. C. Buttre, N. Y.*

23. Mixed. Bust; clean-shaven; directed to the right, facing slightly to the right, looking to the front. Proof, etched in outline. Inscription, centre: *A. Lincoln* [fac. sig.] | *Published by J. C. Buttre*, 48 *Franklin St. New York*—left: *Brady*—right: *Buttre.* $2\frac{9}{16}$ x $3\frac{3}{16}$.

24. Mixed. Bust; beard; directed slightly to the left, facing and looking slightly to the right. $4\frac{1}{2}$ x $5\frac{1}{2}$.

*A*. Proof, etched in outline.

*B.* Finished plate.   Inscription, centre: *A. Lincoln* [fac. sig.]. | *Published by J. C. Buttre,* 48 *Franklin St. New York*—left: *Photo by M. B. Brady* — right: *Engd. by J. C. Buttre, N. Y.*

25. Mixed.   Bust; beard; directed slightly to the left, facing and looking slightly to the right.

$4\frac{1}{8}$ x $5\frac{1}{8}$.

*A.* Proof etched in outline.

*B.* Finished plate.   Inscription, centre: *A. Lincoln* [fac. sig.]—left: *Photo by M. B. Brady*—right: *Engd. by J. C. Buttre, N. Y.*

*C.* Same, printed in red.

*D.* With inscription as before, and underneath in centre: *Abraham Lincoln* | *President of the United States* | *Assassanated April* 14*th,* 1865. | *Published by J. C. Buttre,* 48 *Franklin St. New York.*

*E.* Same, with word "assassinated" corrected.

In *C, D,* and *E,* background has been extended.   This is not the same as No. 24.   The watch-chain is wanting, the shirt-collar is more rolling, there are no buttons on the coat, and there are differences in detail of engraving.

26. Mixed.   Bust; beard; directed to the right, facing and looking very slightly to the right (almost front).   Proof.   Inscription, centre: *A. Lincoln* [fac. sig.]—left: *M. B. Brady.*— right: *J. C. Buttre.*
$5\frac{1}{4}$ x $6\frac{3}{8}$.

27. Line. Bust; beard; directed slightly to the right, facing and looking slightly to the left. Inscription, centre: *A. Lincoln* [fac. sig.] — left: *Photo by M. B. Brady* — right: *Engd. by J. C. Buttre.* $4\frac{1}{4}$ x $4\frac{5}{8}$. Plate, $6\frac{7}{8}$ x $9\frac{7}{8}$.

28. Line and stipple. Bust; beard; directed slightly to the right, facing and looking very slightly to the left (almost front). Proof. Inscription, centre: *A. Lincoln* [fac. sig.] — left: *Brady.* — right: *Buttre.* $3\frac{1}{4}$ x $3\frac{3}{4}$.

29. Line. Bust; beard; directed, facing and looking to the right. Oval (no outline) in rectangular border (no outline); symbolical pictures in the four corners.

 L. P., $7\frac{1}{2}$ x $9\frac{3}{4}$. To outside of border, 10 x $12\frac{1}{4}$.

 *A.* Proof of etching; shadows all indicated.

 > Pen-and-ink note on margin: "No. 2. Etched June 1865."

 *B.* The portrait alone, finished.

 *C.* The full finished plate. Inscription, centre: *Entered according to act of Congress A. D. 1864 by J. C. Buttre . . . New York* | *Engraved and published by J. C. Buttre, 48 Franklin St. New York.* | *A. Lincoln* [fac. sig.] | *Abraham Lincoln* | *16th President of the United States.* | *Assassinated April 14th 1865.* — left: *Border designed by W. Momberger.*—right: *Photograph by M. B. Brady.*

30. Mixed. Full-length, standing; beard; directed slightly to the left, facing and looking slightly to the right. Right hand on table, on which are a bust of Washington, books and papers. Spectacles in left hand. Chair to the right. Inscription, centre: *Published by J. C. Buttre, No.* 48 *Franklin St. New York.* | *Abraham Lincoln* | *President of the United States.*—right: *Abraham Lincoln* [fac. sig.].

$19\frac{1}{2} \times 25\frac{3}{4}$. Plate, $22\frac{1}{4} \times 30$.
See also No. 18.

31. Line. Bust; beard; directed, facing and looking to the right. Oval border. Surrounded by smaller oval portraits of the members of his cabinet. Name of subject appears below, and office above, each portrait. L. P., $1\frac{7}{8} \times 2\frac{5}{16}$.

   *A.* Proof. Etching in outline.

   *B.* Finished plate. Inscription, above, centre: *President;* below, centre: *and Cabinet* 1861. Following contour of oval of bottom (Hamlin's) portrait runs the legend: *Entered according to act of Congress A. D.* 1862 *by J. C. Buttre . . . New York.*

32. Line and stipple. Bust; beard; directed, facing and looking to the left. In oval border. Surrounded by smaller oval portraits of the

Vice-President and seven members and two ex-members of the cabinet.   Lincoln and Hamlin are in the middle (Hamlin above), and the others grouped around them.        L. P., $1\frac{11}{16}$ x $2\frac{4}{16}$.

*A.* Trial proof.   Unfinished.   Faces etched. Dark tone of clothes and shaded background indicated.   Usher and Stanton do not yet appear.   The oval frames are drawn in pencil, as are also small designs between and outside of the ovals, emblematic of the offices of the members of the cabinet.   Behind Lincoln appears the Emancipation Proclamation.

*B.* Trial proof.   Other pencil designs appear; the American flag behind Lincoln.

*C.* The finished plate, with name and office engraved under each portrait.   Inscription, in curved lines, centre: *Entered according to act of Congress in the year* 1864 *by O. D. Case & Co. in . . . Connecticut. | Engraved by J. C. Buttre, New York. | President and Cabinet.*

33. Line and stipple.   Very similar to No. 32, the portraits being placed in the same relative position, although it is not the same engraving. Special points of difference: Lincoln is directed, faced and looking to the right.   Chase's arms are crossed.                L. P., $1\frac{5}{8}$ x $2\frac{1}{8}$.

*A.* Trial proof, etched in outline.

*B.* Trial proof. Clothes worked up and background put in.

*C.* Finished plate, with name and office engraved under each portrait. Inscription, centre, in curved lines: *Entered according to act of Congress A. D. 1865 by O. D. Case & Co. in . . . Connceticut* [sic!] | *Engraved by J. C. Buttre, New York.* | *President and Cabinet.* Inscription and decorative scroll-work are also arranged as in No. 32, yet we have here a different engraving.

### Chubbuck, Thomas.

34. Line and stipple. Bust; beard; directed slightly to the left, facing and looking slightly to the right. Inscription, centre : *Engraved expressly for Holland's " Life of Lincoln."* | *A. Lincoln* [fac. sig.] — right: *Thos. Chubbuck, Engr. Springfield, Mass.*                    $2\frac{3}{4} \times 3\frac{1}{4}$.

### Cole, T.

35. Wood-engraving. Bust; beard; directed to the front, facing and looking slightly to the right. Inscription, left: *Wyatt Eaton* 1877; right: *T. Cole. Sc.*                    $4\frac{15}{16} \times 6\frac{10}{16}$.

### Doney, T.

36. Mezzotint. Bust; beard; directed slightly to the right, facing and looking to the right (almost profile). To the left, books and papers

on a table. Inscription, centre: *Engraved and Published by T. Doney, Esq. | W. Pate, 16 Burling Slip, N. Y.*—underneath, in fac. sig., *yours truly A. Lincoln.*

> " This is . . . based upon a photo by Hesler of Chicago, made in 1860, which was not thought satisfactory because of the unkempt hair; hence Hesler made the 'Ayers' picture, with hair in better order, to suit Eastern patrons."

37. Mezzotint. Three-quarters length; beard; directed to the right, facing and looking to the front. Right arm crooked, forefinger pointing; left arm resting on Emancipation Proclamation on table. Chair and column on the left, portion of curtain on the right. Inscription, centre: *Entered according to Act of Congress in the year 1866 by Thos. Doney (Engraved by T. Doney) in . . . Illinois | Abraham Lincoln.*

$10\frac{3}{4}$ x $13\frac{1}{2}$. Plate, $11\frac{7}{8}$ x 16.

## Fagan, James.

38. Etching. Bust; beard; directed, facing and looking to the right. Remarque proof before letters. In upper left-hand corner: *Published by Rover, Lee & Clem* 1894.

$9\frac{1}{2}$ x $12\frac{1}{4}$. Plate, $11\frac{3}{4}$ x $15\frac{1}{2}$.

## Gugler, H.

39. Line. Bust; beard; directed, facing and looking to the right. Oval, with border of oak

leaves and acorns, in rectangle.   Below, on engraved part, " Lincoln " in large letters.

L. P.,   17 x 21⅝.   Engraved  part,  23 x 29½.
Plate, 26 x 33½.

*A.*  On India paper.   Inscription, centre: *Entered according to the Act of Congress in the
year* 1869 *by John H. Littlefield in* . . .
*the District of Columbia. | Photographic
copyright secured.*— left: *Engraved by H.
Gugler.*— right: *Painted by J. H. Littlefield.*

Signed in pencil: " ɪ. H. Littlefield."

*B.*  On white paper.   Inscription  as  before,
and, underneath, centre: *Published by William Pate and Co.   New York.*


## Hall, A. B.

40.  Line and stipple.   Bust; beard; directed, facing and looking to the right.   Inscription, cen-
tre: *Engᵈ. by A. B. Hall, New York. | A. Lin-
coln* [fac. sig.] | *D. Appleton & Co.*      4 x 5¼.


## Hall, Charles B.

41.  Etching.   Almost full-length, seated; beard;
directed, facing and looking to the right.   Right
hand grasping book resting on right leg crossed
over the left; paper on table at right; mantel
with statuette, other ornaments and portrait in
background.   Inscription, centre: *Etched by*

*Charles B. Hall N. Y.*—left: *Fifty India Proofs only, No.* 16.  4⅝ x 6¼. Plate, 5⁷⁄₁₆ x 7¹⁴⁄₁₆.

42. Etching.  Full-length, seated; beard; directed, facing and looking to the right.  Right hand in lap; left arm resting on arm of chair and against small table. Inscription, centre: *Etched by Charles B. Hall, N. Y.*—left: *Fifty India Proofs only, No.* 16.   3⅞ x 5½. Plate, 5⅝ x 7¾.

### Hall, H. B.

43. Line and stipple.  Bust; beard; directed slightly to the left, facing and looking very slightly to the right (almost front).  The portrait in an oval border (in lower right quarter of the plate) on the top of which is lettered "Abraham Lincoln"; laurel branch below.  To the left is seated Diogenes before his tub, resting left hand, holding lantern, on the frame, and looking down at portrait of Lincoln.  Behind him, base of a large column and a tree; to the left, in distance, the Capitol at Washington. Inscription, centre: *Engd. by H. B. Hall, N. Y.* | *Diogenes his lantern needs no more,* | *an honest man is 'found!—the search is o'er.* | *Entered according to Act of Congress A. D.* 1865, *by N. P. Beers, in* . . . *New York.*

44. Line.  Three-quarters (to below knee), seated; beard; directed, facing and looking to the

right.   Lincoln, wearing spectacles, is looking
at a photograph album held on his knees; his
son "Tad," at his left knee, directed and facing to the front, is looking on with him.   In-
scription, centre:  *Engd. by H. B. Hall.* |
*Abraham Lincoln and his son Thaddeus.* | *Pub-
lished by W. Pate,* 58 & 60 *Fulton St. N. Y.*

$6\frac{5}{8}$ x $7\frac{1}{2}$.   Plate, 12 x 16.

Based on a Brady photo.   See also Nos. 100, 111,
133, 137.

### Hall, H. B., and Sons.

45. Line.   Bust; beard; directed, facing and
looking to the right.   Inscription, in facsimile:
*Your friend, as ever, A. Lincoln;* and, underneath, centre: *Engd. by H. B. Hall & Sons,*
13 *Barclay St. N. Y.*          4 x $4\frac{5}{16}$.

### Hall, H. B., Jr.

46. Line.   Bust; beard; profile to right. Inscription, centre: *Eng'd. by H. B. Hall Jr. from
a Photo. by Brady & Co.* | *Published by Jno.
B. Bachelder.* | *New York.*

$2\frac{1}{2}$ x $2\frac{3}{4}$.   Plate, 9 x $11\frac{1}{2}$.

Published in I. N. Arnold's "Sketch of the Life of
Abraham Lincoln" (1869), with additional lettering.

### Hall (?).

47. Line and stipple.   Bust; beard; profile to the
right.   Proof before letters.   "Private plate."

2 x $2\frac{5}{8}$.   Plate, $4\frac{1}{4}$ x $6\frac{1}{8}$.

## Halpin, F.

48. Line and roulette. Bust; beard; directed to the front, facing and looking slightly to the right. Inscription on plate, left: *From life by F. B. Carpenter*, 1864; right: *Engd. by F. Halpin, N. Y.* Inscription on margin below, centre: *Entered according to act of Congress in the year* 1866 *by F. B. Carpenter . . : New York* | *Abraham Lincoln* [fac. sig.].

$$12\tfrac{3}{4} \times 16\tfrac{7}{8}.$$

## Holcomb and Davis.

49. *A.* Wood-engraving. Full-length, standing; clean-shaven; directed, facing and looking to the front. Left hand on hip, right hand resting on sheet inscribed " Constitutional freedom," lying beside book on table. Signature " Holcomb & Davis Sc." under, and to left of, right foot. Inscription (printed), centre: *Abraham Lincoln* | *President of the United States.*  $12 \times 18\tfrac{1}{2}.$

*B.* Same, with black mourning border. Inscription (in heavier type than in the preceding), centre: *Abraham Lincoln,* | *Late president of the United States,* | *Assassinated April* 14*th,* 1865.

Size to border, $13\tfrac{1}{2} \times 21\tfrac{1}{2}.$

## Hollyer, S.

50. Line and stipple. Bust; beard; directed, facing and looking to the right. Oval, in orna-

mental border.   Inscription, centre, in border:
*Hollyer Eng.* — in margin, below: *A. Lin-*
*coln* [fac. sig.].        $4\frac{1}{4}$ x $5\frac{1}{4}$.   Plate, 7 x 9.

## Jackman, W. G.

51.  Line and stipple.   Bust; beard; directed, facing and looking to the right.   Inscription,
centre: *Engd. by W. G. Jackman, Brooklyn,*
*N. Y.* | *A. Lincoln* [fac. sig.].        $3\frac{5}{8}$ x $4\frac{3}{8}$.

52.  Line and stipple.   To the waist, seated; beard;
directed, facing and looking to the right.   In-
scription, centre: *Abraham Lincoln* | *A. Lin-*
*coln* [fac. sig.] | *Entered according to Act of*
*Congress in the year* 1865, *by Rice, Rutter &*
*Co., in* . . . *Pennsylvania* — left: *Photo by*
*Brady* — right: *Engraved by W. G. Jack-*
*man.*        $3\frac{1}{2}$ x $4\frac{1}{2}$.   Plate, $7\frac{7}{8}$ x $10\frac{7}{8}$.

53.  Line and stipple.   Bust; beard; directed, facing and looking to the right.   Inscription,
centre: *A. Lincoln* [fac. sig.] | *A. Lincoln* |
*Engraved expressly for Abbot's Civil War*
— left: *Photograph by G. D. Appleton &*
*Co.* — right: *Engd. by W. G. Jackman.*

$4\frac{1}{4}$ x $4\frac{3}{8}$.

## Johnson, T.

54.  Etching.   Bust; clean-shaven; directed to the
right, facing slightly to the right, looking to
the front.   Trial proof.   " First state."

$7\frac{5}{8}$ x $10\frac{3}{8}$.   Plate, $9\frac{3}{8}$ x $12\frac{7}{8}$.

Signed in pencil: " T. Johnson, 1899." Plate not yet
finished.

**55.** Etching.   Bust; beard; profile to the left.

9 x 12.   Plate, 11$\frac{3}{8}$ x 14$\frac{1}{2}$.

*A.* Trial proof.   " First state."
Signed in pencil: " T. Johnson."

*B.* Trial proof.   " Second state."
Signed in pencil: " T. Johnson, 1892."

*C.* Trial  proof.   " Third  state."
Signed in pencil: " T. Johnson."

*D.* Finished plate.   " T. Johnson " etched on
left arm.   Inscription on margin, centre:
left: *Abraham Lincoln* [fac. sig.] | *in* 1861,
*Etched for the Republican Club, and dis-*
*tributed at its dinner* | *February* 12*th,* 1892.
*From a Photograph in the possession of L.*
*E. Chittenden* [fac. sig.] — right: *Copy-*
*right,* 1892, *by Thomas Johnson* | *Artist's*
*proof.*

Signed " T. Johnson " in pencil.

**56.** Wood-engraving.   To the waist; almost clean-
shaven, very short side-whiskers; directed and
facing slightly to the right, looking to the
front.   Proof from the original block.

5$\frac{1}{4}$ x 7$\frac{3}{8}$.

Signed in pencil: " T. Johnson."   Said to be from the
earliest known portrait of Lincoln.

**57.** Wood-engraving.   From life mask in profile
to the right, by Douglas Volk.   Proof from
the original block.         3$\frac{11}{16}$ x 4$\frac{7}{10}$.

Signed in pencil: " T. Johnson."

## Jones, R. S.

58. Line. Bust; clean-shaven; directed to the right, facing very slightly to the right, looking to the front. Inscription, centre: (around bottom of oval) *Engd. by R. S. Jones, from a Photograph by Brady* — underneath: *A. Lincoln* [fac. sig.] | *Published by J. Kelly*, 87 *Fulton Street, N. Y.* $3\frac{3}{8}$ x $4\frac{9}{16}$. Plate, 6 x $8\frac{3}{4}$.

## Kruell, G.

59. Wood-engraving. Bust; clean-shaven; directed and facing to the right, looking to the front. Proof from the original block. In upper left-hand corner is engraved: *G. Kruell Copyrighted* 1891. $8\frac{3}{8}$ x $10\frac{7}{8}$.

Signed in pencil: "G. Kruell."

60. Wood-engraving. Bust; beard; directed and facing to the left, looking slightly to the left. Proof from the original block. $8\frac{5}{8}$ x $11\frac{1}{4}$.

Signed in pencil: "G. Kruell."

## Lovett, J. D. (?).

61. Line. Bust; clean-shaven; directed, facing and looking to the right. Oval. To the right is a similar oval, with portrait of Hamlin. Over the portraits and inside the ovals appear, respectively: *A. Lincoln* and *H. Hamlin*. Between the portraits, at the bottom, a bit of field

with fence, and hills beyond. Underneath, two curving branches, under which, to the left: *J. D. Lovett, N. Y.* Over the portraits passes a band lettered *Free territory for a free people,* and at the top appears the American eagle. L. P., $\frac{7}{8}$ x $1\frac{3}{8}$. Plate, $2\frac{3}{4}$ x $4\frac{1}{2}$.

## McRae, J. C.

62. Line and stipple. Bust; beard; directed and facing to the left, looking slightly to the left. Oval, in ornamental frame-design. The whole set in a ruled background, rounded at the upper corners. Underneath the portrait, and projecting below the background, a small panel with picture of " Cabinet Council." Inscription, centre: *A. Lincoln* [fac. sig.] | *Virtue & Yorston, Publishers,* 12 *Dey Street, New York | Entered according to act of Congress by Virtue & Yorston . . . N. Y.*; left: *Engraved by ;* right: *J. C. M<sup>c</sup>Rae.*

L. P., $4\frac{3}{16}$ x 5. To border, $5\frac{15}{16}$ x $7\frac{1}{2}$.

63. Line and stipple. Bust; beard; directed, facing and looking to the right. Inscription, centre: *Engd. by J. C. M<sup>c</sup>Rae, Expressly for Abbott's Civil War. | A. Lincoln* [fac. sig.] | *A. Lincoln.* 4 x $4\frac{1}{2}$.

64. Line. Bust; beard; directed slightly to the left, facing and looking slightly to the right.

Oval, in rectangular border, scenes from Lincoln's life in the four corners, with descriptive lettering. Inscription, centre: *Engraved & published by John C. M^cRae,* 105 *Cedar St. New York.* | *A. Lincoln* [fac. sig.] | *Abraham Lincoln.* | *President of the United States.* | *Assassinated April* 14*th,* 1865.
L. P., 9¼ x 10¾.  To outside border, 10⅝ x 12⅞.

## Marshall, Wm. E.

65. Line.   Bust; beard; directed, facing and looking to the right.   Oval, in rectangular border. In border, below, is engraved: "Abraham Lincoln."   Proof before any letters.

16 x 21.   Plate, 19½ x 25¾.

## Metzmacher.

66. Line.   Bust; beard; directed, facing and looking to the right.

L. P., 7⅝ x 8.   Plate, 8½ x 11¼.

*A.* Proof, with inscription in centre: *Metzmacher, del et sc.,* 1862.

*B.* Finished plate, with inscription, as above, and underneath, centre: *Abraham Lincoln* | (*Président des Etats-Unis*) | *Imprimé & Publié par Goupil, & Cie. Editeurs.   Paris, London, La Haye*—left: *Berlin — Verlag von Goupil & Co.*—right: *New York — Published by M. Knoedler.*

## O'Neill (?).

67. Line. Bust; beard; directed and facing to the left, looking to the front. Inscription, centre: *Abraham Lincoln | Elias Dexter* 562 *Broadway.* 2⅛ x 3⅜. Plate, 6 x 8¾.

## Pelton, O.

68. Line and stipple. Bust; beard; directed to the front, facing and looking slightly to the right. Inscription, centre: *A. Lincoln* [fac. sig.] | *Abraham Lincoln.* | *Assassinated April* 14*th,* 1865 — left: *Photograph by Braddy* [sic!] — right: *Engraved by O. Pelton.* 5½ x 5¾.

## Perine, George E.

69. Line and stipple. Bust; beard; directed, facing and looking to the right. Inscription, centre: *A. Lincoln* [fac. sig.] | *Abraham Lincoln.* | *President of the United States.* | *Engraved Expressly for Headley's History of the Rebellion* — left: *Photograph by Fredricks* — right: *Engd. by Geo. E. Perine, N. Y.*

4⅛ x 4⅜.

70. Mixed. Three-quarters length, seated; beard; directed to left, facing and looking slightly to the right; left hand grasping arm of chair; right hand on Emancipation Proclamation on

table ; curtain in background to left. Inscription, centre : *Entered according to Act of Congress A. D.* 1864, *by Geo. E. Perine. . . . Engraved by Geo. E. Perine, New York . . . New York | Abraham Lincoln* [fac. sig.] | *President of the United States | [*1861–1865*] | Published by George E. Perine, New York.*
8 x 10¾. Plate, 11 x 14¾.

## Perine and Giles.

71. Mixed. Three-quarters length, seated; beard; directed to the left, facing and looking very slightly to the right. Right hand resting on Emancipation Proclamation on table, left one on arm of chair. Curtain in back, from left to behind the head. Inscription, centre : *Engraved for the Eclectic by Perine & Giles, N. Y. | A. Lincoln* [fac. sig.] | 16*th President of the United States.* 4⅞ x 6⅞. Plate, 7 x 9¼.

## Pound, D. J.

72. Line and stipple. Half-length, standing; clean-shaven; directed to the right, facing slightly to the right, looking to the front. Inscription, centre : *Engraved by D. J. Pound from a Photograph | President Lincoln.*
4⅞ x 6¼.

73. Line and stipple. Three-quarters length, standing; clean-shaven; directed to the right, facing slightly to the right, looking to the front. Right

hand at side, left hand resting on two books on table. Curtain at the left. Inscription, centre: *Engraved by D. J. Pound, from a Photograph by Brady of New York | Abraham Lincoln, | President of the United States. | The drawing room portrait gallery of eminent personages | Presented with the Illustrated News of the World | 125 Fleet Street.* 7½ x 11.

"Photo by Brady, made in N. Y. in 1860, Feb'y, the basis of many of the pictures of Lincoln published in the East in the campaign of 1860."

## Rajon, Paul.

74. Etching. Bust; clean-shaven; directed and facing to the right, looking to the front. Proof with remarque (sketch of cast of Lincoln's hand). 7¾ x 9⅞. Plate, 9¾ x 12¾.

Signed in pencil: " Rajon."

## Ritchie, A. H.

75. Mixed. Bust; beard; directed very slightly to the left, facing and looking to the right. Inscription, centre: *Abraham Lincoln.* | *16th President of the United States* — left: *Photo. by Brady* — right: *Engd. by A. H. Ritchie.*

9½ x 11. Plate, 13½ x 17½.

76. Line and stipple. Half-length, standing; beard; directed, facing and looking to the left; right hand at side, left one behind back. Inscrip-

tion, centre : *Engd. by A. H. Ritchie.* | *Abraham Lincoln.*                    4 x 6½.

77. Line and stipple.    Half-length, standing; beard; directed slightly to the left, facing and looking slightly to the right.    Right hand at side, left one behind back.    Inscription, centre : *Entered according to act of Congress, A.D. 1865, by Derby & Miller, . . . New York.* | *A. Lincoln* [fac. sig.] | *Engraved by A. H. Ritchie expressly for Raymond's Life of Lincoln.* | *Published by Derby & Miller, New York.*    4¼ x 6½.

78. Line.    Full-length, standing; beard; directed, facing and looking to the left.    Right hand grasping cloak wrapped around him ; left hand resting on table, on which are sheets inscribed " Constitution," " Union," and " Proclamation of Freedom," and several volumes with title " Jefferson's Works " erased, so as to be barely, discernible.    Globe and flag to the left.    Proof before letters.    19¾ x 26¼.    Plate, 22⅜ x 30⅝.

> The original plate was a portrait of Calhoun, Lincoln's head being subsequently inserted and the title "Jefferson's Works " obliterated.

### Roberts, W.

79. Wood-engraving.    Bust; beard; directed to the right, facing very slightly to the right, looking to the front.    In circle, at head of text of " Proclamation of Emancipation."    The latter

is printed within an ornamental border, in which are three vignettes on each side (showing life of slave on the left, and of the free negro on the right) and view of Fort Sumter burning, at bottom (the whole $14\frac{3}{4}$ x $19\frac{1}{2}$). Inscription below, centre: *Entered according to Act of Congress, in the year* 1864, *by R. A. Dimmick, in* . . . *New York* — left: *W. Roberts, Del. sc.* — right: *C. A. Alvord, Printer.*

L. P., $2\frac{3}{8}$.

## Rogers, J.

80. Line. Three-quarters length, seated; beard; directed to the left, facing and looking to the front. Arms resting on arms of chair. Inscription, centre: *J. Rogers sculpt.* | *A. Lincoln* [fac. sig.]. $4\frac{3}{8}$ x $6\frac{3}{16}$.

## Sartain, John.

81. Mezzotint. Bust; beard; directed to the front, facing and looking slightly to the right. Oval. Inscription, centre: *Published by R. R. Landon, agt.* 88 *Lake St. Chicago, Ill.* | *Engraved by John Sartain, Phila.* | *A. Lincoln* [fac. sig.].

$4\frac{5}{8}$ x $5\frac{3}{4}$.

82. Mezzotint. Bust; beard; directed slightly to the left, facing and looking slightly to the right. Inscription, centre: *Entered according to the Act of Congress in the year* 1865, *by Bradley & Co.* . . . *Pennsylvania* | *Bradley*

*& Co. Publishers, 66 Nth. 4th St. Philadelphia
| Abraham Lincoln —* left: *After Photo : ᵹrom
Life —* right: *Engraved by John Sartain.*

8⅞ x 10½.   Plate, 12 x 16⅛.

83. Mezzotint and line.  Three-quarters length,
seated; beard; directed slightly to the left,
facing and looking to the right.  Left hand
resting on document on table, right hand
grasping quill pen.  At right, foot of statue
treading on broken fetters.  Inscription, centre:
*Entered according to Act of Congress, in the
year* 1864, *by E. D. Marchant, . . . Pennsyl-
vania | Abraham Lincoln | 16th president of
the United States | From the Original Portrait
by E. D. Marchant | Painted at the White
House in* 1863 *and now in tne* [sic!] *Posses-
sion of the Union League of Philadelphia |
Bradley & Co. Publishers 66 North Fourth
St. Phila.—* left: *After the original picture
painted ᵹrom life —* right: *Engraved by John
Sartain, Phila. | Abraham Lincoln* [fac. sig.].

10 x 13.   Plate, 13 x 17.

84. Mezzotint.  Full-length, seated; beard; directed to the left, facing and looking to the
front.  Right hand, with quill pen, resting on
table, on which are a bust of Jackson, lamp,
books, newspaper, etc.  Globe, and roll inscribed " Campaign of 1864," to the right.

Inscription, centre: *Published by R. R. Landon,
Agt., 88 Lake St. Chicago, Ill.* | *Abraham Lincoln*
| *President of the United States* — left: *The
head after a Photograph 'from life, the Picture
by Boyle* | *Proof.*— right: *Engraved by John
Sartain, Phila.*                     $15\frac{1}{4}$ x $21\frac{1}{2}$.

85. Mixed. Full-length, standing; beard; directed, facing and looking to the right; left
hand on table. Inscription, centre: *Published
by William Smith, No. 702 So. 3d St. Phila.*
| *Engraved by John Sartain, Phila.* | *Abraham
Lincoln* | *President of the United States.*
$13\frac{7}{8}$ x $20\frac{1}{4}$.   Plate, $15\frac{3}{4}$ x $24\frac{1}{2}$.

## Sartain, Samuel.

86. Mixed. Half-length, seated; beard; directed
to the left, facing very slightly to the left,
looking to the front. Left hand, holding folded
paper, resting on arm of chair; curtain at back.
Oval in rectangular border. Inscription,
centre: *Entered according to act of Congress in
the year* 1864, *by S. Sartain, in . . . Pennsyl-
vania.* | *Abraham Lincoln.* | *Published by Rice
& Allen, corner Burdick & Water Sts., Kala-
mazoo, Mich.*— right: *Engraved by Samuel
Sartain* | *Printed by Irwin & Sartain.*
Oval, $8\frac{1}{8}$ x $10\frac{3}{4}$.  To outside of border, 10 x $12\frac{1}{2}$.
Plate, $12\frac{3}{8}$ x $16\frac{3}{8}$.

87. Companion piece to the preceding.  Portrait of Mrs. Lincoln.  Mixed.  Half-length, seated; directed to the front, facing and looking to the right.  Both hands in lap, right one holding closed fan.  Curtain and column in background.  Inscription, centre: *Entered according to act of Congress in the year 1864, by S. Sartain in . . . Pennsylvania. | Mrs. Abraham Lincoln. | Published by Rice & Allen, 90 State St. Chicago, Ill.*—right: *Engraved by Samuel Sartain. | Printed by Irwin & Sartain.*
Oval, 8⅛ x 10¾.  To outside border, 10 x 12½.
Plate, 12½ x 15⅞.

88. *A.* Mixed.  Bust; clean-shaven; directed slightly to the right, facing very slightly to the right, looking front.  Oval, in rectangle.  Inscription, centre: *Engraved by Samuel Sartain, after the miniature from life by J. Henry Brown, in the possession of Judge Read. | A.  Lincoln* [fac. sig.] | *Published by James Irwin, 728 Sansom St. Philadelphia.*    4 x 5⅜.    Plate, 7¼ x 10.

*B.* Same, with beard added.  Background reworked.  After " A. Lincoln," the inscription now changed to: *16th President of the United States. | Published by Sam! Sartain, 726 Sansom St. Philadelphia.*

## Sartain, William.

89. Mixed.  Bust; beard; directed to the left, facing and looking almost directly to the front.

Back of chair indicated. Oval, in rectangular border. Inscription, centre: *Engraved & Published by William Sartain, 728 Sansom St. Philada.* | *Abraham Lincoln.* $8\frac{7}{8}$ x $10\frac{7}{8}$.

90. Mixed.. Bust; beard; directed, facing and looking to the right. Inscription, centre: *Engraved & published by William Sartain, 728 Sansom St. Phila.* | *Abraham Lincoln.*
$9\frac{1}{2}$ x $11\frac{1}{8}$. Plate, 12 x 15.

91. Mixed. Three-quarters, standing; beard; directed to the front, facing and looking slightly to the right. Left hand resting on books on table. Column to the right. Inscription, centre: *Entered according to Act of Congress in the year* 1866, *by William Sartain . . .* | *Published by William Sartain.* | *Abraham Lincoln* | — right: *Engraved by William Sartain* | *A. Lincoln* [fac. sig.]. 14 x $18\frac{1}{8}$. Plate, $17\frac{1}{2}$ x $22\frac{3}{4}$.

**Serz, J.**

92. Line and stipple. Full-length, seated; beard; directed, facing and looking to the right. Left hand grasping paper and resting on table, on which are a Bible, another book and inkstand. Quill pen in right hand. Column, with bust of Washington to the right. Eagle over bookcase in background. Inscription, centre: *Published by John Dainty, Phila.* | *Abraham Lincoln* | *President of the United States* | *Sign-*

*ing the Emancipation Proclamation | Entered according to Act of Congress, in the year* 1864, *by John Dainty . . . Pennsylvania.* — left: *Painted by W. E. Winner.* — right: *Engraved by J. Serz.* | *Proof.*          14⅛ x 18½.

## Smith, H. Wright.

93. Mixed.  Bust; beard; directed and facing to the right, looking to the front.  Inscription, centre: *H. Wright Smith.* | *A. Lincoln* [fac. sig.] | *Published by Benj. B. Russell,* 515 *Washington St. Boston.*   3½ x 3½.   Plate, 7 x 8¼.

94. Line and stipple.  Bust; beard; directed, facing and looking to right.  Inscription, centre: *A. Lincoln* [fac. sig.] | *Late president of the United States* | *New York, D. Appleton & Co.* — left: *Miller & Mathews Photors.* — right: *H. W. Smith, N. Y.*          3⅞ x 4¾.

95. Line and stipple.  Bust; beard; directed and facing to the right, looking slightly to the right. Inscription, centre: *H. W. Smith, N. Y.* | *A. Lincoln* [fac. sig.] | *Entered according to Act of Congress in the year* 1875, *by S. Walker & Co. . . . at Washington.*          6 x 7⅜.

96. Line and stipple.  Bust; beard; directed slightly to the right, facing and looking almost to the front.  Inscription, centre: *H. W.*

*Smith, Sc.* | *A. Lincoln* [fac. sig.] | *S. Walker, Boston.* $6\frac{1}{2}$ x $8\frac{1}{8}$.

## Stuart, F. T.

97. Stipple. From a sculptured bust; beard; directed slightly to the left; head in profile, to the left. Inscription, left: *Jones Sc.*—right: *F. T. Stuart Eng. Boston.* 2 x $3\frac{1}{4}$.

> "The bust was modeled from life by Thos. D. Jones, Columbus, O."

## Stueler, H.

98. Mixed. Bust; beard; directed, facing and looking to the right. Inscription, centre: *Published by J. C. Buttre Co.* | *Abraham Lincoln* [fac. sig.] — right: *Engd. by H. Stueler.*
$3\frac{3}{4}$ x $4\frac{1}{2}$. Plate, 7 x 10.

## Walter, A. B.

99. Mixed. Bust; beard; directed and facing to the right, looking very slightly to the right (almost front). Inscription, centre: *Engraved by A. B. Walter, Philada.* | *Hon. Abraham Lincoln,* | *President of the United States* — right: *A. Lincoln* [fac. sig.]. $4\frac{1}{2}$ x $5\frac{7}{8}$.

100. Mixed. Lincoln and "Tad," as in No. 68 (which see), but showing more of legs. Oval, in rectangular black border. Inscription,

centre: *Published by Bradley & Co. 66 Nth
4th St. Philadelphia | President Lincoln and
his son "Tad"* — left: *After a photo 'from
life* — right: *engraved by A. B. Walters.*

9 x 10⅜.   Plate, 13 x 14¾.

**Weger.**

101. Line and stipple.   Bust; clean-shaven; di-
rected to the left, facing and looking very
slightly to the left (almost front).   Inscrip-
tion, centre: *Abraham Lincoln | Verlag v.
Baumgärtner's Buchh.*— left: *Nach einer
Photographie v. Brady* — right: *Stich u.
Druck v. Weger, Leipzig.*

4½ x 4¼.   Plate, 6¼ x 8½.

# GROUPS.

**Buttre, J. C.**

102. Mixed.   Lincoln Family.   All full-length.
Lincoln at right; beard; directed and facing
to the left, looking down at book held on his
crossed knee, " Tad " at his side.   Mrs. Lincoln at left.   Table between, in front of which
sits Willie, and behind which Robert is
standing.        25⅜ x 17⅞.   Plate, 28¾ x 21½.

*A.* Trial proof, not finished.

*B.* Finished plate. Proof.  Inscription below,
centre: *Entered according to act of Congress*

*A. D.* 1867 *by J. C. Buttre in . . . New York.*

C. Print. The upper corners now rounded off. Inscription, centre: *Entered according to act of Congress in the year* 1873 *by J. C. Buttre in . . . Washington.* | *Published by J. C. Buttre,* 48 *Franklin St. New York.* | *The Lincoln family in* 1861 — left: *Painted by F. B. Carpenter* — right: *Engraved by J. C. Buttre.* The names of the members of the family also appear under their respective portraits.

103. Line. Trial proof. " Lincoln and Stephens in Hampton Roads, Feb. .6/65." Lincoln, Hunter, Campbell, Stewart, Stephens and Seward (in order named, beginning at left) seated around a small table. $6\frac{9}{16}$ x $4\frac{5}{16}$.

**Kelly, Thomas (?).**

104. Mixed. Lincoln Family. All full-length. Lincoln at the right, seated; beard; directed, facing and looking to the left; left hand holding book. Mrs. Lincoln at the left, Thomas (" Tad ") standing by her side. Table between, behind which stand Robert and Willie. In background: left, column; right, curtain; centre, view of dome of Capitol at Washington. Inscription, centre: *Entered*

*according to Act of Congress A. D. 1866 by Thos. Kelly, in . . . N. Y. | Lincoln Family. | Published by Thomas Kelly, 264 Third Avenue, between 22d & 23d Sts. N. Y.* The names of the members of the family also appear under their respective portraits.

24$\frac{7}{8}$ x 18.   Plate, 28$\frac{3}{4}$ x 21$\frac{5}{8}$.

## McRae, J. C.

105. Line and stipple.   Lincoln and the drummer boy.   Upper corners rounded.   Inscription, centre: *Entered according to Act of Congress in the year 1867, by F. Heaton, in . . . Ohio. | F. Heaton, publisher, Cleveland, O. | Lincoln and the drummer boy. | " The boy advanced . . . for me." | . . . —* left: *Painted by Knapp —* right: *Engd. by J. C. M$^c$Rae, N. Y.*

12$\frac{7}{8}$ x 16$\frac{1}{2}$.   Plate, 17 x 21$\frac{3}{4}$.

## Ritchie, A. H.

106. Mixed.   "The first reading of the Emancipation Proclamation before the cabinet."   Lincoln seated at a table, his legs crossed, paper in his left hand, surrounded by the members of his cabinet.   Names of the personages are printed in margin below their respective portraits.   Inscription, under title above given, centre: *From the original picture painted at the White House in 1864. | Entered according to act of Congress in the year 1865, by F. B. Carpenter in . . . New York | Premium En-*

*graving 'from "The Independent"* — left:
*Painted by F. B. Carpenter* — right: *En-graved by A. H. Ritchie.*    21 x 32½.

### Robin, A.

107. Mixed. Lincoln and Family. At right, Lin-coln seated (directed and facing to the left), with a book on his lap, from which he looks up and very slightly to the left; "Tad" at his right side, a table at his left elbow. Facing him is Mrs. Lincoln, seated, with Robert, in uniform, standing at her left side. Picture of Willie hanging over Lincoln's head. Oval. Inscription, centre, following bottom of oval: *Engd. by A. Robin, N. Y.  Entered according to act of Congress, in the year* 1869, *by G. W. Massee in . . . Pennsylvania* — below, in straight line: *Lincoln and'family.*  8⅛ x 10⅛.

### Sadd, H. S.

108. Mixed. Lincoln, full-length; beard; standing in centre, directed to the front, facing and looking almost to the front (very slightly to the right). Quill pen in right hand, left hand resting on sheet inscribed "Constitution of the United States of America," placed on a column and under a bust of Washington, with laurel wreath around head. On the left, Gen. Scott and Henry Clay seated, others standing. On the right, Webster (with right

hand resting on the "Constitution" before mentioned) and others standing — Gen. Butler in background — and one seated, holding shield with colors of U. S.   In foreground, right: crown and sceptre on the floor; centre: drapery.   At the top, right: eagle drawing aside drapery.   Over Lincoln's head, female genius with branch in left hand and liberty-cap on pole in right.   At top, left, clouds, with winged genius on globe inscribed: "America."   Inscription, centre: *Union.* | *Published by William Pate, 58 & 60 Fulton St. N. Y.* | *Boston, L. A. Elliot & Co.—* left: *Painted by T. H. Matteson —* right: *Engraved by H. S. Sadd.* | *Printed by W. Pate.*                                    19½ x 26½.

> "This plate was originally made in 1850–1 to commemorate the Compromise Measure. Calhoun was the central standing figure. In 1861 Lincoln's head was substituted. Gen. Butler was also substituted."

## Sartain, John.

109. Mixed.   Lincoln received by the spirit of Washington.   Both in clouds, surrounded by angels.   Inscription, centre: *Entered according to Act of Congress in the year 1866 by W. H. Hermans in . . . New York.* | *Published by W. H. Hermans Penn Yan Yates Co. N. Y.* — left: *Designed by W. H. Hermans.* | *Artist's proof —* right: *Engraved by John Sartain, Phila.*      14 x 18¼.   Plate, 17¾ x 23.

### Sartain, William.

110. Mixed. Lincoln Family. Lincoln and "Tad" on the left, Mrs. Lincoln on the right, all seated; table between, behind which stands Robert, back of whom hangs picture of Willie. "Artist's proof." Inscription, centre: *Entered according to Act of Congress, in the year* 1866, *by William Sartain in . . . Pennsylvania.* | *Published by Bradley & Co.* 66 *N. Fourth St. Philadelphia.* | *R. H. Curran, Rochester, New York* — left: *Painted by S. B. Waugh* | *Proof* — right: *Engraved by William Sartain* | *Printed by Irwin & Sartain.* 25 x $17\frac{7}{8}$. Plate, $22\frac{1}{4}$ x 28.
Signed "William Sartain" in pencil.

### Walter, A. B.

111. Mixed. Lincoln Family. Lincoln and "Tad" as in No. 45 (which see), but carried out to full length; Mrs. Lincoln seated at left, Robert, in uniform, standing behind them. Picture of Willie in upper right-hand corner. Inscription, centre: *Published by John Dainty, Philadelphia.* | *Prest. Lincoln and family.* | *Entered according to Act of Congress in the year* 1865 *by John Dainty in . . . Pennsylvania* — left: *Painted by F. Schell* — right: *Engraved by A. B. Walter.* 10 x $13\frac{3}{8}$.

4

# LITHOGRAPHS.

## PORTRAITS.

112. Bust; beard; directed, facing and looking to the right. *A. Lincoln* in facsimile on tinted portion, lower right-hand corner. Inscription underneath, centre: *Verlag v. A. Janke & Simon. Berlin Ritter-Str.* 100 | *A. Lincoln.* | *President of the United States of America.*

$9 \times 10\frac{1}{8}$.

113. Bust; beard; directed to the left, facing and looking to the front. Inscription, centre: *Abraham Lincoln.* | *Copied by permission from the original picture by Matthew Wilson —* | *now in possession of Hon. Gideon Welles, Secy. of the Navy.* | *Published by L. Prang & Co., Boston, Mass.* | *Entered according to Act of Congress in the year* 1865 *by L. Prang & Co. in . . . Massachusetts.*   $9\frac{3}{4} \times 11\frac{3}{4}$.

**114.** Bust; beard; directed to the front, facing and looking to the right. Oval. Inscription, centre: *Abraham Lincoln | Issued from Buf-*'*fords' Print Publishing House,* 313 *Washington St. Boston, Mass. | Entered according to Act of Congress in the year* 1865 *by J. H. Buffords, in . . . Mass.*    10¼ x 12¼.

**115.** *A.* Bust; beard; directed and facing very slightly to the right, looking to the front. Inscription, centre: *Abraham Lincoln —* right: *Published by William Smith,* 702, *South Third St., Philada.*    18½ x 23½.

    *B.* Same, rounded off below top button of vest, colored. Black background. No inscription.    18½ x 22.

**116.** Bust; beard; directed to the left, facing and looking very slightly to the right. Oval; face, background and border tinted. Inscription, centre: *Abraham Lincoln, | Sixteenth President of the United States —*left: *Though shrined in dust our President now lies | The memory of his deeds shall ever bloom | Twined with proud laurels shall the olive rise | And wave unfading o'er his honored tomb.—*right: *To him the nation yields undying fame | First on her heroes' list inscribe his name | High o'er the sculptured marble let him stand | The un-selfish Patriot of his native land.*    17¾ x 21½.

**117.** Bust; beard; directed, facing and looking to the right. Oval; tinted. Inscription, within the border: *A. Lincoln* [fac. sig.] — underneath, centre: *Abraham Lincoln,* | *Late President of the U. S. Assassinated April 14th 1865.*        $10\frac{7}{8} \times 14$.

**118.** Bust; beard; directed, facing and looking slightly to the left. Inscription, centre: *Abraham Lincoln* | *the late President of the United States of America* | ✚ | *15th April* 1865. | *Verlag v. Seitz, Hamburg.*        $7\frac{1}{2} \times 9$.

**119.** Half-length, seated; beard; directed to the left, facing and looking to the front. Right arm apparently resting on arm of chair, hand holding quill pen; left hand on lap. Inscription, centre: *Abraham Lincoln.*        $8 \times 12$.

**120.** Description of this tallies with that of No. 119, but it is not the same lithograph. The former is darker in the hair, which is also higher, and there are other points of difference. Inscription, centre: *Abraham Lincoln.*
$7\frac{7}{8} \times 11\frac{3}{4}$.

**121.** Chromo. Three-quarters length, seated; beard; directed and facing to the right, looking very slightly to the right. Right arm resting on arm of chair, left one on table, next to red book. Red curtain at left, on bottom of which is printed: *Oelfarben-Druck & Verlag | Berg & Porsch, Berlin.* No other inscription.

$14\frac{3}{4}$ x 18.

122. Three-quarters length; standing; beard; directed slightly to the right, facing and looking to the right. Right hand thrust into breast of coat, left hand resting on Emancipation Proclamation lying on table, on which is also placed a high hat, behind which appears the top of a cane. Top part of a chair to the left, and curtain above. In background on the right is seen the Capitol at Washington. Inscription, centre: *Abraham Lincoln. | Issued from Buffords Print Publishing House, 313 Washington St. Boston.* $8\frac{1}{2}$ x $11\frac{1}{4}$.

123. Full-length, standing; clean-shaven; directed to the left, facing and looking very slightly to the left. Right hand on paper on table, left hand on hip. Inscription, centre: *Magee, 316 Chesnut* [sic!] *St. Phila. | Abraham Lincoln | Entered according to Act of Congress, in the Eastern District of Pennsylvania, by J. Magee, in the year* 1861. $3\frac{7}{8}$ x $7\frac{1}{2}$.

124. Full-length, standing; beard; directed, facing and looking to the front. Left hand on hip, right hand resting on sheet inscribed " Constitution. Freedom," on table, on which are

placed also books, a lamp, a globe with lettering "America," etc. Column and curtain
in background on left. Chair behind figure, with three books on the floor beside it.
A large rug takes up most of the floor space.
Inscription, centre: *Abraham Lincoln* —
right: *A. Lincoln*. [fac. sig.]. 19 x 24⅝.

125. Bust; clean-shaven; directed very slightly to
the right, facing and looking to the right.
Inscription, centre: *Yours truly A. Lincoln*
[fac. sig.] | *Hon. Abraham Lincoln* — right:
*J. H. Bufford's, Boston.* 15¾ x 22.

> "Painted by Thomas Hicks." Probably drawn on
> the stone by J. E. Baker.

126. Colored. Half-length, seated; beard; directed, facing and looking to the right. Corner of table with book at right. At bottom,
near centre, "J. Baker" is lithographed on
arm of chair. No other inscription.

18¾ x 23½.

> "After the Brady ('64) photo."

127. Bust; beard; directed, facing and looking to
the right. In black oval border, decorated
above with shield bearing U. S. colors, below
with flag of U. S., both in colors. *Max Ro-
senthal Del* is lithographed inside the border,
at the left, on the right arm. Inscription,

centre: *Abraham Lincoln | Sixteenth President of the United States | Born February* 12, 1809. *Died April* 15, 1865. *| Published by L. N. Rosenthal, | No.* 327 *Walnut St. Phila. Pa.* 9¾ x 12¼.

128. To the waist, seated; beard; directed to the left, facing and looking to the front. Right hand thrust into vest, left arm resting on arm of chair and holding book. Curtain and base of column in background. Black mourning border. Inscription, centre: *Entered according to Act of Congress in the year* 1861, *by Currier & Ives, in* . . . *New York | Abraham Lincoln. | Sixteenth President of the United States | Assassinated April* 14*th,* 1865.

8⅜ x 11⅜.

129. Bust; beard; directed to the front, facing and looking to the left. In oval border, placed in centre of " Proclamation of Emancipation " executed in ornamental penmanship, with five small designs interspersed. Inscription, centre: *Entered according to act of Congress by A. Kidder in* . . . *Illinois* — left: *Designed & executed by A. Kidder Publisher. office* 429 *Broadway N. Y. 86 Dearborn St. Chicago. | Lith. & printed by Chas. Shober Cor. Clark & Lake St. Chicago.*

L. P., 2½ x 3.

130. Bust; beard; directed, facing and looking to the right. The sheet is covered with the written " Emancipation Proclamations," certain portions of which are heavily shaded and thus form a dim picture of the President. The whole is set in an ornamental border, which encloses also in each corner at the bottom a design representing, respectively, the negro ill-treated in the South in " 1860 " and freed by the North in "1865." Inscription, centre: *Allegorical portrait of | Abraham Lincoln. | Respectfully dedicated to the Union Leagues of the United States by the Publishers | Published by the Art Publishing Association of Philadelphia ; Swander Bishop & Co. | Entered according to Act of Congress in the year* 1865, *by Swander Bishop & Co. in . . . Pennsylvania* — left: *Des. & Drawn with a Steel pen by R. Morris Swander* — right: *Engraved facsimile by P. S. Duval & Son Philada.* $15\frac{7}{8}$ x $21\frac{1}{8}$.

131. Full-length, standing; beard; directed to the front, facing and looking slightly to the right. Left hand on hip, right one on paper lying on table. Placed in centre of Emancipation Proclamation, written around the figure. Floral border above and below. Inscription, centre: *The original | Designed and Executed | entirely with a | Pen | by | Gilman R.*

*Russell* | *Prof of Penmanship.* — left : *P. S. Duval & Son lith. Phila.* — right : *Published by a Company.* 17½ x 25½.

132. Bust; beard; directed, facing and looking to the left. Oval to the right. On left side is a similar portrait, in oval, of Washington, directed and facing to the right, looking to the front. Between the portraits, an eagle, figure of Justice, Capitol (under which the title " The champions of freedom "). In left lower corner, Revolutionary soldiers; in right lower corner, Union soldiers; etc., etc. Inscription, underneath, centre : *Entered according to Act of Congress in the year* 1865, *by Samuel Marshall in . . . Delaware* — left : *Bradley & Co., Publishers No.* 66 *N.* 4. *St. Philada.* —right : *P. S. Duval & Son lith. Phila.*

L. P., 7⅜ x 9⅜.

133. Lincoln and Tad, as in No. 45, but more shown of the legs. Oval, in an ornamental, rectangular border. Tinted. To the right, part of signature, beginning with " Y," cut off at oval line. Inscription, below, centre : *Abraham Lincoln, the martyred president.* | *Assassinated, April* 14*th,* 1865 — left, in the border : *Pub. by John Smith,* 756 *So.* 4*th St. Phila.*

18⅝ x 23¾.

4 *

# GROUPS.

**134.** Outbreak of the Rebellion.  Davis and Southerners on left, in uproar and tearing American flag; Lincoln on right, addressing supporters of the Union; Columbia in the centre, with a figure of Justice militant.  Inscription, centre: *Entered according to Act of Congress A. D. 1865, by Kimmel &* *Forster in . . . New York.* | *The outbreak of the Rebellion in the United States 1861 —* right: *Kimmel & Forster, N. Y.*  24½ x 17.

**135.** The Council of War.  Signed *P. Krämer*, at bottom, near the right corner.  Inscription, centre: *Entered According to Act of Congress A. D. 1865 by N. P. Beers in . . . N. Y.* | *The council of war* | *" I propose to fight it out on this line if it takes all summer." | U. S. Grant* [fac. sig.].  The names of Porter, Farragut, Lincoln, Sherman, Thomas, Grant, and Sheridan, who compose the " Council," are printed under the picture.    18¾ x 14.

**136.** Lincoln and his Family.  Lincoln, seated, on the right, hands resting on book (" Constitution of the United States ") on leg; wife and the two boys on the left.  Table between, behind which stands Robert in uniform.  To the right, pedestal with bust of Washington.

In background, arcade, with curtains, giving distant view of water and hills. Inscription, centre: *Published by William Smith, Printseller, no. 702 South Third St. Philada. | Lincoln and his ?family.* — left: *From an Original Drawing by Ad. Biegemann* — right: *lih* [sic !] *D. Wiest.* 24 x 18.

137. Lincoln Family. On left, Lincoln and Willie as in "Lincoln and Tad," No. 45, but carried out to full length; Robert standing behind Lincoln's chair. On the right, Mrs. Lincoln, seated; "Tad" on low stool beside her. Table in centre. Inscription, centre: *Entered according to Act of Congress in the Year 1865 by Wm. C. Robertson, in . . . New York. | Abraham Lincoln & family | Respectfully Dedicated to the People of the United States* — left: *Designed & drawn by H. A. Thomas* — right: *Published Imp. Wm. C. Robertson, 12 Ann St. N. Y.* 16½ x 13¼.

138. Freedom to the Slaves. Negro kneeling, kissing left hand of Lincoln, whose right hand points upward, while his right foot treads on broken fetters. Negro woman and two children in back. Inscription, below, centre: *Freedom to the slaves | Proclaimed January 1st 1863 , by Abraham Lincoln, President of the United States. | "Proclaim liberty throughout*

*All the land unto All the inhabitants thereof."*
*—Lev. xxv.* 10.——left: *Pubd. by Currier*
*& Ives—*right: 152 *Nassau St. N. Y.*
$8\frac{1}{2}$ x $11\frac{1}{2}$.

139. Grand Reception . . . Numerous portraits of
celebrities of the time. In foreground, Lin-
coln introducing Mrs. Grant to Mrs. Lincoln.
Within border and on the lithograph appears:
*Lith. of Major & Knapp,* 449 *Broadway,*
*N. Y.* Inscription, below, centre: *Entered*
*according to Act of Congress in the year* 1865
*by Frank Leslie in* . . . *N. York.* | *Grand re-*
*ception of the notabilities of the nation,* | *at the*
*White House* 1865. 20 x $14\frac{3}{4}$.

140. Death-bed of Lincoln. In the right lower
corner of the lithograph appears: *P. Krä-*
*mer, Del,* reversed. Inscription, centre:
*Entered According to Act of Congress A. D.*
1865 *by N. P. Beers in* . . . *N. Y.*—left:
*Printed by A. Brett & Co.* 83 *Nassau St.* |
*Proof—*right: *Published by Jones & Clark*
83 *Nassau St. N. Y.* Underneath are printed
the names of the personages surrounding the
bed. $18\frac{5}{8}$ x $24\frac{3}{4}$.

141. Lincoln, supported by Father Time and an
angel, is borne upward on clouds out of his
tomb, which is lettered: *A. Lincoln,* | *Died*

*April* 15th 1865. In foreground, an Indian and a genius of America, with armor, shield, eagle, etc. Figures of women and children in background to left. Signature *D. Wiest* in lower left-hand corner. Inscription, centre: *Published by William Smith, Printseller No. 702 South Third St. Phila. | In memory of Abraham Lincoln. | The reward of the just.*

$18\frac{1}{4}$ x 24.

142. " Home of Abraham Lincoln." Tinted. Blue sky. Inscription, centre: title as above — left: *L. Prang & Co. lith. Boston.* $13\frac{3}{8}$ x 11.

---

143. Process plate. Line. Bust; beard; directed, facing and looking to the right. Placed in upper half of large sheet headed *The Autobiography of Abraham Lincoln*, the autobiography appearing below in facsimile of Lincoln's writing. Inscription, underneath, centre: *Entered according to Act of Congress in the year* 1872 *by Jesse W. Fell, in . . . Washington | Published by James R. Osgood & Co. Boston.* L. P., $7\frac{3}{4}$ x $9\frac{1}{8}$.

144. Process plate. Bust; beard; directed, facing and looking to the right. Inscription, centre: *Abraham Lincoln* — left: *copyright* 1894 *by the Taber Art Co.* — right: *painted by Cyrus Cobb.* 14 x 17.

145. Process plate. Reproduction of bas-relief. Bust; clean-shaven; directed slightly to the right, facing and looking to the right (almost profile). Inscription, top, centre: *Abraham Lincoln* — top, left: *MDCCC | IX* — top, right: *MDCCC | LXV* — left, near bottom: *H. H. | Zearing | Sculpt | Chicago | '92* — right lower corner: *Copyright* 1892.      7 x 9.

# DRAWINGS
# AND MISCELLANIES.

**146.** Oil-painting in black-and-white by F. B. Carpenter. For description, see No. 48, F. Halpin's engraving of this.

**147.** Lincoln Family. Oil-painting in black-and-white by F. B. Carpenter. For description, see No. 102, J. C. Buttre's engraving of this.

$36\frac{1}{2}$ x 27.

**148.** Abraham Lincoln entering Richmond. Black-and-white drawing by Thomas Nast. Lincoln (with beard, wearing high hat and long frock coat) accompanied by escort of sailors and surrounded by enthusiastic negroes. Signed *Th : Nast* 1/68. In lower right corner: *Lincoln entering Richmond, Va., April 4th, 1865.*                     18 x 24.

Owned by Union League Club, N. Y.

149. Lincoln at Willard's Hotel. Black-and-white drawing by Pierre Morand. Full-length, standing; beard; directed to the left, head in profile to the left. Lincoln at window with shade pulled down, wearing high hat, resting elbows on sill, right hand holding roll of paper, legs crossed. In lower left corner is written *At Willard's June* 1864. $3\frac{7}{8}$ x 7.

150. Black-and-white drawing by Massard, "About 1865." Bust; beard; directed, facing and looking to the right.

Drawn part measures $4\frac{15}{16}$ x $6\frac{14}{16}$.

151. Water-color drawing by David Hunter Strother (*Porte Crayon*). Full-length, standing; beard; directed to the front, facing and looking to the left. Wearing high hat and long blue coat; right hand holding umbrella, left hand outstretched. Signed "D. H. S." in lower right corner; "at Richmond, 1865 | 9 April" in lower left corner. $3\frac{11}{16}$ x $7\frac{1}{16}$.

152. "Abraham Lincoln in the War Office." Black-and-white by David Hunter Strother (*Porte Crayon*). Full-length, standing; beard; directed and facing to the left, looking to the front. Wearing high hat, left hand holding paper, right grasping umbrella. "Map of Virginia" at top, to right. Signed "D. H. S."

in lower right corner; "1864" in left lower corner. $2\frac{13}{16} \times 6\frac{4}{16}$.

153. Original block engraved by G. Kruell.
(See No. 59 for description.) $9\frac{1}{2} \times 13$.

154. Bronze circular bas-relief by C. Calverley. Bust; beard; profile to the right. Inscription, around circle: *Abraham Lincoln Feb · 12 · 1809. April · 14 · 1865.* At bottom: *C. Calverley. 1898. Copyright.* Diameter, $10\frac{3}{4}$.

155. Plaster-of-Paris bas-relief by Charles Calverley. Head; beard; profile to the right.
Rectangular, $14\frac{3}{4} \times 19\frac{1}{4}$.

"Original model for the marble bas-relief executed for the Union League Club, 1869."

156. Medal of bronze, gilded. Head; beard; profile to the left. Inscription on circumference: *Dédié par la démocratie française à Lincoln Président deux fois élu des États-Unis —* underneath head: *Franky Magniadas.* On the reverse, a tomb; a winged female genius on the left, with an anchor and a bale of goods; on the right, two half-naked negroes, one with musket and bayonet. To the right, ballot-box labeled "vote." At top, American eagle with the usual symbols (shield, arrows, branch, and band inscribed "e pluribus unum") surrounded by stars and rays. In background, a ship at the left, a locomotive at the right. Inscrip-

tion on tomb: *Lincoln l'honnête homme | abolit l'esclavage rétablit l'union | sauva la République | sans voiler la statue de la liberté | il fut assassiné le 14 avril | 1865*. Underneath, in straight line: *Franky-Magniadas* — following curve of medal: *liberté — égalité — fraternité*.                Diameter, 3½.

Said to have been got up, by subscription, by French workmen.

157. Bronze life mask of Lincoln by L. W. Volk. Inscription on the back: *This cast was made for R. W. Gilder, a subscriber to the fund for the purchase and presentation to the United States Government of the original mask made in Chicago, April, 1860, by Leonard W. Volk from the living face of Abraham Lincoln. This cast was taken from the first replica of the original in New York City, February, 1884.*

158. Bronze cast of Lincoln's hands by L. W. Volk. Inscription on each hand: *Copyright 1886 by Leonard W. Volk. This cast of the hand of Abraham Lincoln was made from the first replica of the original made at Springfield, Ill., the Sunday following his nomination to the presidency in 1860.*

159. Group of 14 photographs, on a number of which most of the known engraved portraits of Lincoln are based.

Lightning Source UK Ltd.
Milton Keynes UK
UKHW012016021218
333216UK00014B/2437/P